ORIGIN OF THE COSMIC BATTLE

Harrison House Books by Joseph Z

Demystifying the Prophetic: Understanding the Voice of God for the Coming Days of Fire

Servants of Fire: Secrets of the Unseen War & Angels Fighting for You

Breaking Hell's Economy: Your Guide to Last-Days Supernatural Provision

Breaking Hell's Economy Study Manual

Jesus and the Kingmakers

Origin of the Cosmic Battle

ORIGIN OF THE COSMIC BATTLE

JOSEPH Z

© Copyright 2024– Joseph Z

Printed in the United States of America. All rights reserved. No portion of this book may be reproduced, stored in a retrieval system, or transmitted in any form or by any means—electronic, mechanical, photocopy, recording, scanning, or other—except for brief quotations in critical reviews or articles, without the prior written permission of the publisher. Unless otherwise identified, Scripture quotations are taken from the New King James Version. Copyright © 1982 by Thomas Nelson, Inc. Used by permission. All rights reserved.

Scripture quotations marked NIV are taken from the HOLY BIBLE, NEW INTERNATIONAL VERSION®, Copyright © 1973, 1978, 1984, 2011 International Bible Society. Used by permission of Zondervan. All rights reserved.

Scripture quotations marked KJV are taken from the King James Version.

All emphasis within Scripture quotations is the author's own.

Published by Harrison House Publishers
Shippensburg, PA 17257

ISBN 13 TP: 978-1-6675-0950-1
ISBN 13 eBook: 978-1-6675-0951-8

For Worldwide Distribution, Printed in the U.S.A.
1 2 3 4 5 6 7 8 / 28 27 26 25 24

CONTENTS

	Introduction	1
1	Celestial Hierarchies and Angelic Origins	3
2	Becoming the Prince of Darkness	19
3	Prison Planet	31
4	Hell Is Not Enough	39

INTRODUCTION

One of the reasons this book became a reality is partly due to a visitation I had several years ago. An angelic encounter occurred after finishing a two-week series on my morning live broadcast in which I taught about angels. The messenger came to share seasonal information with Heather and me regarding our personal lives, the future of our ministry, what we were to expect, and some clear orders. This experience left me in tears and sent me on a journey to write this book.

I have long believed that the way angels are depicted and interacted with is not the highest and best use of why they exist. They are not deities; they are not something to be worshiped or even revered. They are *fiery servants* who minister to the *heirs of salvation*. They are not for us to fellowship with and command to do whatever we desire. As *flames of fire* who serve the saints, it should be understood that they are not butlers or errand runners for Christians. Instead, they are fiery servants activated and empowered by the Voice of God. Angels are not arbitrary beings that float in and out of our lives based on a whim. They are servants, flames of fire, potentially created out of the presence of God, the Consuming Fire.

Understanding the origins, storyline, and the fall of their mutinous brothers is crucial. This knowledge, along with the guidelines by which angels operate, will provide you with a deeper understanding of the spirit realm, the origins of angels, the different ranks of angels, and the profound reasons why hell is not enough for the crime that was committed. I hope that by the end of this book, the information provided will reveal God's love and how His rescue plan has paved the way for escaping the same fate as the enemy.

Chapter One

CELESTIAL HIERARCHIES AND ANGELIC ORIGINS

For our God is a consuming fire.

—Hebrews 12:29

God is a consuming *fire!* Angels are fiery servants. I believe angels were created and drawn directly out of God's essence. Imagine these fiery flames pulled directly out of the Consuming Fire Himself—forged by His Word and operating as *autonomous extensions* of Himself!

Additionally, these are called *winds*. Wind represents God's breath, and these winds are also an extension of His breath! Winds are closely associated with God's breath or voice.

The voice of the Lord divideth the flames of fire.
—Psalm 29:7 KJV

When the Lord speaks, He is speaking according to Psalm 29 and dividing these winds and flames of fire. *Dividing* carries the connotation of commanding or releasing them on assignment. Angels were created right from the very presence of God and are part of His *fiery DNA*. They have their thoughts and will; however, being birthed straight from the fire of God, they are to do what they are *built for*.

Angels might also be considered highly intelligent spiritual beings not destined to be united with a human body. Unlike God's creation of man, these spiritual beings do not have a human soul but live out an immortal lifespan due to not possessing a physical body. Angels are spirits created to be God's companions in the kingdom of heaven. Therefore, it was a terrible travesty when many of these created ones, in the beginning, *participated in Lucifer's mutiny!* That must have hurt the heart of God as these creations of His were violating their very purpose and acted in complete betrayal of what they were built for.

CAN ANGELS STILL REBEL?

Angelic beings are fascinating, and we don't completely grasp them because the Word of God only gives us glimpses of their behavior and operations. One example would be asking: How is it that angels once fell from grace? What assurances are there that the current forces of heaven would not do what their former companions did when they rebelled against God? The Word of God doesn't give us exact clarity on this issue, yet we get glimpses into how angels might respond to the temptation of receiving glory for themselves.

When exposed to an angelic messenger in Revelation 19, John the Revelator fell down and began to worship the angel. In a dramatic response, the angel urgently said, "See that you do not do that! Worship God!" A glimpse of insight is revealed here. The Bible refers to an innumerable number of angels who still serve God; there was a smaller group of them who were deceived into rebelling against Him.

Of the many who remained, they had the opportunity to witness the judgment pronounced on the rogue angels; it stands to reason that they had extreme clarity of the consequences for unrighteous acts of disobedience—gloomy dungeons, some buried, some placed into outer darkness. Even the angels imprisoned right now under the river Euphrates for the *day of judgment*, mentioned in the book of Revelation, must have garnered the attention of the loyal hosts of heaven. Any doubt was indeed canceled out when they witnessed the creation of hell and knew the location of the second death, *the lake of fire.*

These angelic warriors and messengers also witnessed the Church of Jesus, which can bind and loose spiritual forces in heaven and earth, not to mention casting out demons and so much more. I believe those who witnessed the rebellion and stood with integrity by the Lord God Almighty are thankful to the point of fear, knowing what they would have been sentenced to had they followed the same path as their wicked brothers. If there is any thought of rebellion among angels today, it is undoubtedly met with the reality of the punishment and fate they are privy to regarding fallen angels who left their proper abode. We will investigate more of this throughout the pages ahead.

Angelic ranking and order are revealed in the Scripture. It likely offers insight into how God's kingdom operates, much like a government with a military and police force. It could be that the purpose of many angelic and celestial beings was to oversee creation from the spiritual side of reality. This is recognizable even in Lucifer's life before he gained the moniker Satan. He was the anointed cherub who covered. Ezekiel 28:14 (KJV), "Thou art the *anointed cherub* that covereth; and I have set thee so: thou wast upon the holy mountain of God; thou hast walked up and down in the midst of the stones of fire."

CELESTIAL HIERARCHIES

Authority and position were part of the differing celestial beings. Today, these positions remain in God's kingdom. What each position does and how it operates are only shown in small snapshots throughout Scripture. We know the Lord has established His kingdom structure with various authorities and celestial responsibilities.

> *Far above all principality and power and might and dominion, and every name that is named, not only in this age but also in that which is to come.*
>
> —Ephesians 1:21

> *For by Him all things were created that are in heaven and that are on earth, visible and invisible, whether thrones or dominions or principalities or powers. All things were created through Him and for Him.*
>
> —Colossians 1:16

Referencing these two passages of Scripture shows *five different ranks*. Dionysius (a theologian from AD 500) fixed their number and order. He laid out what he called *celestial hierarchies*, in which angelic entities were arranged into three hierarchies containing three choirs each, in the order of *seraphim, cherubim, and thrones; dominations, virtues, and powers; principalities, archangels, and angels*. He concluded that only the last two choirs have an immediate mission to men. In the Middle Ages, Dionysius' *speculative doctrine* was taken over and developed by others; a treatise on angels became a part of the commentaries on the *Sentences* of Peter Lombard from the 13th century onward.

Thomas Aquinas (theologian 1225–1274) taught an interesting point of view regarding the angelic will, meaning their choices and decisions. Aquinas, after much study and consideration, concluded that one good or bad act by an angelic entity *fixes him irrevocably in good or evil*. This must have been in reference to the original decision they were presented with to do good or evil. Additionally, most historical scholastics taught that the angels were created at the same time as the material universe and that they were *elevated to a state of grace* in order to undergo a test followed either by supernatural beatitude or eternal damnation; furthermore, that the divine mysteries, even the incarnation, were then revealed to them.[1]

Fascinating would be one way to describe the possibility of Aquinas' conclusions regarding angelic choices and Dionysius' *celestial positions!* It is interesting to ponder whether angels deciding to do good or bad is an original decision that sets the course of their eternal destiny. As these early theologians concluded, righteous angels could have known they had chosen wisely after witnessing what happened to their mutinous brothers. As a result, they likely became fully persuaded by the light of God. As to what the rank and file might be in the unseen realm, we can only go as far as the Word of God does. To fully embrace Dionysius' *celestial positions* view would require a *level of speculation*, but it is still worth looking at. One thing we can stand on firmly is references to angelic figures Scripture does speak of.

The following is a list of the references spoken of in Scripture.

Seraphim

Above it stood seraphim; each one had six wings: with two he covered his face, with two he covered his feet, and with two he flew. ³ And one cried to another and said: "Holy, holy, holy is the Lord of hosts; The whole earth is full of His glory!" ⁴ And the posts of the door were shaken by the voice of him who cried out, and the house was filled with smoke. ⁵ So I said: "Woe is me, for I am undone! Because I am a man of unclean lips, And I dwell in the midst of a people of unclean lips; For my eyes have seen the King, the Lord of hosts." ⁶ Then one of the seraphim flew to me, having in his hand a live coal which he had taken with the tongs from the altar. ⁷ And he touched my mouth with it, and said: "Behold, this has touched your lips; Your iniquity is taken away, and your sin purged."

—Isaiah 6:2-7

Cherubim

After he drove the man out, he placed on the east side of the Garden of Eden cherubim and a flaming sword flashing back and forth to guard the way to the tree of life.

—Genesis 3:24 NIV

Thrones

…whether thrones or dominions or principalities or powers.

—Colossians 1:16

Dominion

Far above all principality and power and might and dominion….

—Ephesians 1:21

Powers

…whether thrones or dominions or principalities or powers.
—Colossians 1:16

Principalities

Far above all principality and power and might and dominion….

—Ephesians 1:21

...whether thrones or dominions or principalities or powers.

—Colossians 1:16

Archangels

For the Lord Himself will descend from heaven with a shout, with the voice of an archangel, and with the trumpet of God. And the dead in Christ will rise first.

—1 Thessalonians 4:16

Yet Michael the archangel, in contending with the devil, when he disputed about the body of Moses, dared not bring against him a reviling accusation, but said, "The Lord rebuke you!"

—Jude 1:9

Angels

And of the angels He says: "Who makes His angels spirits and His ministers a flame of fire."

—Hebrews 1:7

But to which of the angels has He ever said: "Sit at My right hand, till I make Your enemies Your footstool"? [14] Are they not all ministering spirits sent forth to minister for those who will inherit salvation?

—Hebrews 1:13-14

ORIGIN OF THE COSMIC BATTLE

Entities of Higher Substance

All created things—including spirit beings such as angels, cherubim, seraphim, and each referenced in this chapter—are a form of spiritual material substance. Some of these substances may potentially be of a higher form than others. Though it would seem that all are visible in their realms or dimensions—when applying our understanding, the human experience of only seeing and perceiving our three-dimensional space—some of these dimensional spaces may not be visible to others of lower realms.

Spirit beings, for example, are of a higher substance than flesh and the ordinary, corporeal material we can see. They are not limited to natural substances as we know them. Higher substance beings can go through closed doors, walls, and any material object. This is seen throughout Scripture and even in testimonies.

I'm grateful for the late Chuck Missler's observations on dimensions. The following are the 10 known dimensions.

> Space is not simply an empty vacuum. Isaiah 64:1 says it can be torn; Psalm 102 says it can be worn out like a garment; Hebrews 12:26, Haggai 2:6, and Isaiah 13:13 say it can be shaken; in 2 Peter 3:12, it

can be "burnt up"; in Revelation 6:14, "it split apart like a scroll." Hebrews 1:12 says it can be "rolled up like a mantle." What is meant by "rolled up"? Let's think that through: in order for space to be rolled up, there must be some dimension in which it's thin. (If it's not thin, you can't roll it up.) Also, if it can be rolled up, it can be bent. If it can be bent, there must be some direction toward which it can be bent. The whole idea of being rolled up implies thinness and an additional dimension in which to roll it up, which begins to indicate that space has more than three dimensions, which we now know today from particle physics.

But the Scripture has said all along that we have additional, spacial dimensions. Nachmanides, a Hebrew sage of the twelfth century, concluded from studying Genesis, chapter 1, that the universe has ten dimensions. Four of those are directly "knowable" and six of them are "not knowable" (in his vocabulary). Particle physicists in the 21st century now believe that the universe has ten dimensions but only four of them are directly measurable.

The possibility of these ten dimensions and the potential spiritual activity that may vary within them is fascinating. After all, according to the reference by Missler, regarding 21st century particle physicists—the universe indeed has ten dimensions that we know about. Could certain spiritual beings be limited to their dimension and only able to see beneath them? This concept is interesting because, according to Scripture, we know that the prince of this world was cast out.

When Jesus was about to go to the cross, He said in John 12:31, "Now is the judgment of this world; now the ruler of this world will be cast out." From where was the ruler of this world cast out? The courts of heaven. You see the devil coming before the Lord with the angels to present themselves before Him. Satan had this access because it had been given to him by Adam and Eve when he deceived them. This was one of the main reasons Jesus came! To destroy the works of the devil!

For this purpose the Son of God was manifested, that He might destroy the works of the devil.

—1 John 3:8

This logically leads us to the question: Does this apply to the realm of darkness and the fallen angels? Ephesians 6, written after Jesus knocked the devil out of his access to heaven, references this:

For we do not wrestle against flesh and blood, but against principalities, against powers, against the rulers of the darkness of this age, against spiritual hosts of wickedness in the heavenly places.

—Ephesians 6:12

In which you once walked according to the course of this world, according to the prince of the power of the air, the spirit who now works in the sons of disobedience.

—Ephesians 2:2

Although the devil doesn't have full access to heaven as he once did, he and the fallen angels, along with the demonic hordes, have a specific position on earth. These seats of authority will not be entirely removed until the Lord returns and binds the devil for a thousand years and ultimately sentences him to the lake of fire.

What does this mean for the ranks of darkness today? They are likely fallen mirrors of angelic servants of light, only much less powerful and far weaker as they no longer align with the Lord of heaven. As we listed several types and ranks of angelic, celestial beings in the kingdom of God, it very well could be that their counterparts function with the same mode of operation in the kingdom of darkness.

They don't have power by the name of Jesus or the authority that believers, covered under the blood of Jesus,

ORIGIN OF THE COSMIC BATTLE

possess. They have territories, hearts, and minds under their persuasion, which has proved effective throughout history.

When we recognize that we wrestle not against flesh and blood but against principalities, powers, and rulers of wickedness in high places, what we are dealing with is their evil influence on free moral agents and giving these principalities and powers the ability to make decisions and run nations through their "hosts." Preaching the gospel is the highest and most potent form of breaking these strongholds, and after that comes the renewing of the mind! The best form of long-term deliverance is excellent Bible teaching.

When approaching the idea that there might be angelic beings in different classes or positioned apart from one another throughout these ten dimensions, this leads to interesting speculation. One thing we do know is that the vast majority of humans will not see beyond their natural five senses until they cross into eternity upon death. Most of humanity will remain limited to this three-dimensional experience, never encountering the other seven dimensions beyond them.

> *For I am persuaded that neither death nor life, nor angels nor principalities nor powers, nor things present nor things to come, ^{39} nor height nor depth, nor any other created thing, shall be able to separate us from the love of God which is in Christ Jesus our Lord.*
>
> —Romans 8:38-39

What is the conclusion about ranks and levels of angelic, celestial authority? The answer remains the same—preach the gospel, win as many as you can, and make disciples by the Word of God! Understand that when praying and walking out what God has assigned you to do in this life, you cannot be separated from the great love of God!

NOTES

1 Cross and Livingstone, The Oxford Dictionary of the Christian Church, s.v. "angel," https://www.oxfordreference.com/display/10.1093/acref/9780192802903.001.0001/acref-9780192802903-e-295?rskey=2IRCHC&result=295.
2 Chuck Missler, *Learn the Bible in 24 Hours* (Nashville, TN: Thomas Nelson, 2011), 17-18.

Chapter Two

BECOMING THE PRINCE OF DARKNESS

In the beginning…

—Genesis 1:1

When considering the creation of the universe, there is much to be *deciphered*. I will present a possible narrative in story form that explains why the devil came into existence—from Lucifer to Satan. It is short and colorful, but I believe it will drive the point home.

A Brief Story of Creation

At the very beginning, before time was measurable, before stars, mountains, and seas, before man was on the planet, I imagine an epoch in which the Creator of all things was looking far into the distance, His thoughts were fixed, and the sense of destiny was palpable. I imagine one of the angelic hosts standing near Him, asking, "Lord, what are You gazing at in such a captivated manner?"

"You will see," replied the great God of the universe.

At this statement, the sons of God knew something was happening and began gathering together. Something was undoubtedly stirring. There was excitement in the air; something was happening that they had never witnessed in all of their existence. The *Ancient of Days* stepped forward with His attention directed at the void stretched out before them all. He paused, then spoke, "Stars be!" and stepping forward, He swung His arm in a sweeping motion from left to right while simultaneously opening His powerful hand and flinging a variety of burning lights far out into the void. Each light found its place, brightened, and shone from deep within the void.

When the sons of God saw the radiant lights throughout the void, they shouted with joy! They had never seen anything like this. He looked at them, smiled, and said, "Do you like it?"

"Yes!" they cried.

He said, "It's all still moving out there—it will continue expanding forever."

With this knowledge, all the angels' eyes became intent with expectation.

Turning His attention to a closer area of this starry void, He began to create. His demeanor and approach were much like an artist painting on a canvas. His focus and gaze were fixed on a particular area as He began to place planets, moons, meteors, and a specific star in a localized space. He called the single star the *sun,* and the other prominent light named the *moon.* Upon this nomenclature, His audience of angels went wild!

He then turned to them all, saying, "Watch!" Suddenly, as if zooming in on a map, they all went from the void of space to hovering above a water-covered planet. The Lord began calling dry land "Appear" and aquatic life "Be."

Land creatures of all sizes—birds, giraffes, and herds of wild stallions—suddenly ran across the open plains. Shouting and praises once again erupted among the sons of God! They began jumping up and down, releasing exuberant shouts of joy and praising God. A moment like this had never happened before, and these sons of God were overwhelmed by what they witnessed.

> *When the morning stars sang together, and **all the sons of God shouted for joy?***
>
> —Job 38:7

About this time, one of the prominent angels was flying by. This entire event had captured his attention; he was intrigued by all the activity. He landed near the Lord and the angels standing on the earth. At this moment, the

ORIGIN OF THE COSMIC BATTLE

Lord of Hosts, the God of Creation, the Great I AM, said, "I've saved the best for last…."

The Lord kneeled and placed His hands into the dirt. The prominent angel was suddenly captivated by this moment and asked, "What are You doing?"

"You will see," replied the Lord, with great pleasure on His countenance. His mighty hands began forming an image from the dirt into which He had placed His hands; He was creating a body—a man.

Lucifer, the angel asking questions, said, "I don't like this!"

The Lord paid no attention to Lucifer's statement and continued until, finally, He opened the mouth of this dirt figure, and as He did, the great God of the universe breathed in deeply with one magnificent breath—then He released His very essence into the newly molded soil. The soil suddenly inhaled, eyes opened, and the dirt began to stand to its feet—now alive.

Lucifer examined this new being called man. He quickly and impatiently studied everything about this dirt figure now standing and breathing. Suddenly, he stepped back with horror. His face filled with disgust as he looked at God, the Father, and said, "This thing reminds me of something. It walks and talks. It is made of lowly dirt, yet it reminds me of something."

The Lord said, "What is it?"

Lucifer replied, "It reminds me of, I can't help but notice...no...it cannot be, how!?" Now visibly shaken, Lucifer cried out, "This is not possible. It's only dirt! *It reminds me of You!*"

God said, "Why yes, this is My son. His name is Adam."

And God said, Let us make man in our image, after our likeness: and let them have dominion over the fish of the sea, and over the fowl of the air, and over the cattle, and over all the earth, and over every creeping thing that creepeth upon the earth. ²⁷ So God created man in his own image, in the image of God created he him; male and female created he them.

—Genesis 1:26-27 KJV

Lucifer had a realization at this moment, a realization of what had just transpired. He recognized that God had just placed His breath and image within the dirt. What this meant for Lucifer was that God had just placed dirt above him! Dirt was now exalted above Lucifer! Psalm 8:4-5 says that man was made a little lower than the angels. However, the actual Hebrew word the translators used was *Elohim*, a Hebrew word translated as "God" more than 2,600 times in the Old Testament that designates the one true God.

What is man that You are mindful of him, and the son of man that You visit him?⁵ For you have made him a little

ORIGIN OF THE COSMIC BATTLE

lower than the angels, and You have crowned him with glory and honor.

—Psalm 8:4-5

Lucifer's Rage

At that moment, Lucifer, now trembling with rage, cried out! *"How dare You! How could You! I hate it! I will kill it!"* Because of this, war broke out as Lucifer began to explain to many angels that God had demoted them from their rightful place. Michael, the warring archangel, gathered angels faithful to God the Father and collided with the rebellious horde of angels who went rogue.

Michael and his angels cast them out of their access to heaven. Thus began the saga of light versus darkness, with humankind in the balance. The epic levels of violence, atrocities, and evil experienced throughout history stem from this moment. It is sad to realize that God did not create Adam to endure such things. He was created for fellowship, for family. When the Lord walked with Adam in the cool of the day, He built a relationship with Adam. His plan was never to see evil come upon creation or on His son and daughter, Adam and Eve. The good news is God was not outmatched and cannot be outwitted. Jesus would come one day as the Last Adam and change everything.

Lucifer's Contempt

Of judgment, because the ruler of this world is judged.
—John 16:11

Lucifer's contempt was something he birthed in his heart from the beginning of his existence. Jesus called the devil "a murderer from the beginning" and "the father of liars" in John 8:44. In the book of Revelation, John the apostle makes it abundantly clear that the dragon mentioned is "that serpent of old" also known as the devil or Satan.

*So the great dragon was cast out, that **serpent of old**, called the Devil and Satan, who deceives the whole world; he was cast to the earth, and his angels were cast out with him.*
—Revelation 12:9

*He laid hold of the dragon, that **serpent of old**, who is the Devil and Satan, and bound him for a thousand years.*
—Revelation 20:2

The devil led a conflict that erupted among the angelic ranks within heaven's armies, and it was all over humanity. It is fascinating to consider that these angelic beings believed Lucifer over God to the point that war erupted. This thought has often led me to ask, "Why would God allow this? How is it that these angels could think in this fashion?" Students of the Word of God can see why the devil was so angry.

Let's consider a passage from Job 1, in which Satan comes before God among the "sons of God." The term "sons of God" is the Hebrew word *b'nai Elohim* and implies that these angels are God's direct creations. This refers to the angels present before God's throne. The same reference is used again in Job 38:7 when *the sons of God shout for joy at the creation of the world*.

Angels enjoyed the status of being direct creations of God the Father Himself. There was nothing like them until He created the first man. Adam was also a direct creation of God, but that is not all! Adam was made in God's image and likeness because he had the very breath of God within him! This set him apart from the angels who, although they were themselves direct creations of God, did not carry His image and likeness as Adam did. As a result, this may have been the main point the devil used to accuse God to the angels who believed his lies. We will discuss the ramifications of their rebellion in the pages ahead.

The Beginning

In the beginning was the Word, and the Word was with God, and the Word was God.

—John 1:1

Before we explore angels further, let's go back to the beginning momentarily. It must have been astonishing in the beginning! Just imagine it.

God in "eternity past" thinking about you. There was peace, stillness, and fulfillment. God, the great I Am should be as the other time it is written. the Great I AM, most likely had never experienced sorrow or an angry thought up to this time. He considered the future within His inner image, marinating what would come. Greater clarity is shown to us in John 1:1, where Scripture speaks of "eternity past" using the terminology, "the Word was with God." This phrase "was with" is the Greek word *pros*, which means "toward," and in this case, it means "toward one another" or "face to face." Another way of saying it would be that God the Father and the pre-incarnate Son looked into each other's countenance throughout "eternity past." What were They thinking about? I believe They possibly were planning the existence of creation and the dramatic story arc of mankind.

Scripture reveals that Jesus was going to be crucified ever since the foundation of the world. Revelation 13:8 says Jesus was "The Lamb slain from the foundation of the world." Think about that! God the Father and Jesus the Son knew not only what was within each other, but They knew that mankind would fall, that angels would rebel, and that the only way of redemption would be Jesus offering Himself.

They knew this from the foundation of the world! More amazingly, They created it all despite the issues that would surely come. Why? Because They wanted to know you.

> *Looking unto Jesus, the author and finisher of our faith, who for the joy that was set before Him endured the cross, despising the shame, and has sat down at the right hand of the throne of God.*
>
> —Hebrews 12:2

Additionally, the Son knew that from Him (God the Father) to Him and through Him are all things. Thus, the Son would only do what He saw His Father doing.

> *For of Him and through Him and to Him are all things, to whom be glory forever. Amen.*
>
> —Romans 11:36

JESUS—THE VOICE OF GOD

The Father is the Source, the One who loves the Son and through Him would love all that would come in "eternity future." It must have been a pleasant moment for Them when the time came to manifest what They had imagined together. The inner essence of the Father desired to create what was already a reality on the inside. There was only one way to release it—to speak. His voice was found in His Son. The worlds would be formed through Jesus because He is the exact representation of God the Father—especially in word form.

In my mind, I see it like this: "Let there be light!" was uttered, and the sound of that voice came through the Son, and light was. Jesus, the Word made flesh. Jesus was that same "Word with God" in the beginning. Jesus was the "Master Craftsman" beside God the Father, creating the world. The Father speaking through the Son, crafting the world. Jesus is the Voice of God!

*The Lord possessed me at the beginning of His way, before His works of old. ²³ I have been established from everlasting, from the beginning, before there was ever an earth. ²⁴ When there were no depths I was brought forth, when there were no fountains abounding with water. ²⁵ Before the mountains were settled, before the hills, I was brought forth; ²⁶ while as yet He had not made the earth or the fields, or the primal dust of the world. ²⁷ When He prepared the heavens, I was there, when He drew a circle on the face of the deep, ²⁸ when He established the clouds above, when He strengthened the fountains of the deep, ²⁹ when He assigned to the sea its limit, so that the waters would not transgress His command, when He marked out the foundations of the earth, ³⁰ then **I was beside Him as a master craftsman**; and I was daily His delight,*

rejoicing always before Him, [31] rejoicing in His inhabited world, and my delight was with the sons of men.
—Proverbs 8:22-31

It is profound to realize that from the time of creation through the Son to the moment of jealousy and rage that filled Lucifer, God the Father, and Jesus the Son had a rescue mission in place to redeem man. From man's fall to redemption, God, knowing everything that would transpire, still chose to move forward with creation and the plan for "eternity future"!

The angels saw it all; they observed every scenario between the divine Father and the fallen creation. On each side of the issue, both good and evil, these angelic entities are woven into the narrative, having a part to play in this cosmic saga. Curiosity or contempt are issues depending on which angelic messengers are involved.

CHAPTER THREE
PRISON PLANET

It is fascinating to consider the devil and all the fallen ones. These angels who left their proper abode are, likely, bound to earth. It has become a prison planet for them. No longer can these enter the realms of heaven or the courts of the Lord. What is left for them to contemplate is a fiery end. *Judgment awaits these*, yet it is plausible to believe they live in self-deception, thinking they will defeat the righteous and lay claim to this earth. After all, Lucifer cried out, saying he wanted all the worship!

> *How you are fallen from heaven, O Lucifer, son of the morning! How you are cut down to the ground, you who weakened the nations!* [13] *For you have said in your heart: "**I will** ascend into heaven, **I will** exalt my throne above the stars of God; **I will** also sit on the mount of the congregation on the farthest sides of the north;* [14] ***I will** ascend above the heights of the clouds, **I will** be like the Most High."*

—Isaiah 14:12–14

ORIGIN OF THE COSMIC BATTLE

Go to the Word of God regarding what I am about to say. Keep the main thing the main thing. Whenever we take steps into arenas of speculation, we mustn't force an issue and do what biblical studies label *eisegesis*—the idea that people inject their ideas, beliefs, and philosophies into the Scripture rather than extracting what the Scripture is saying. This doesn't mean we cannot or should not consider looking into the possibilities. This is what we will do when looking into the following scripture. Ezekiel 28 references what many scholars would agree is a passage regarding the devil. Let's read the following reference and consider the possibilities:

> ***You were in Eden****, the garden of God; every precious stone was your covering: the sardius, topaz, and diamond, beryl, onyx, and jasper, sapphire, turquoise, and emerald with gold. The workmanship of your timbrels and pipes was prepared for you on the day you were created. *¹⁴* You were the anointed cherub who covers; I established you; you were on the holy mountain of God; **you walked back and forth in the midst of fiery stones***. *¹⁵* You were perfect in your ways from the day you were created, till iniquity was found in you. *¹⁶* **By the abundance of your trading** you became filled with violence within, and you sinned; therefore I cast you as a profane thing out of the mountain of God; and I destroyed you, O covering cherub, from the midst of the fiery stones. *¹⁷* Your heart*

was lifted up because of your beauty; you corrupted your wisdom for the sake of your splendor; I cast you to the ground, I laid you before kings, that they might gaze at you. ¹⁸ You defiled your sanctuaries by the multitude of your iniquities, by the iniquity of your trading; therefore I brought fire from your midst; it devoured you, and I turned you to ashes upon the earth in the sight of all who saw you. ¹⁹ All who knew you among the peoples are astonished at you; you have become a horror, and shall be no more forever.

—Ezekiel 28:13-19

First, it reads, "You were in Eden." This cannot be talking about anyone else but Lucifer. Only three individuals were present in Eden—Eve, Adam, and the serpent. There is much conjecture about the serpent. I take the conventional view that the serpent is indeed Lucifer, becoming Satan because Adam and Eve gave him their position and seat of authority.

Second, notice it says, "You walked back and forth in the midst of the *fiery stones*." This is possibly a reference to the planets in our solar system.

Third, Ezekiel tells us iniquity was found in Lucifer. How? By the abundance of his trading. Why would it say, "the abundance of his trading"? It could be that before the fall, he was handling commerce on Earth; and the moment humanity was created, he realized his position as

ORIGIN OF THE COSMIC BATTLE

the cherub who covered or oversaw this planet (or all the planets, aka "the stones of fire") was suddenly diminished. Lucifer was put out of a job. Jealousy and rage took over, which caused him to rebel and destroy all of God's new rulers of Earth from Eden.

Fourth, Lucifer was cast down, as referenced in Ezekiel 28. Jesus, of course, makes mention of this moment:

And He said to them, "I saw Satan fall like lightning from heaven. ¹⁹ Behold, I give you the authority to trample on serpents and scorpions, and over all the power of the enemy, and nothing shall by any means hurt you."

—Luke 10:18-19

Jesus says, "I saw Satan fall like lightning," His powerful statement regarding the devil being cast out, but then adds, "I give you authority to trample on serpents and scorpions and over all the power of the enemy, and nothing shall by any means hurt you."

In the same moment, Jesus tells the disciples He witnessed Satan's fall and continues by putting that instance into the same category as the authority we have been given over snakes, scorpions, and all the power of the enemy. Again, He might be referencing when these fallen angels, their demon cohorts, and all the power they collectively possessed likely fell to earth with Satan. Demons themselves were likely added to the mix later.

A fierce battle over Earth may be because all these evil and dark forces have no other place to influence except Earth! *It is like a close-quarters arena; these wicked beings want the territory.*

PRISON RULES

Outside of God's kingdom, these evil entities play by prison rules, meaning anything they can do to enslave mankind is what they will do! The devil and all his forces are limited to a set of rules. Their rules are territorial. Whatever is given to them is done by influencing the mind and, ultimately, by cooperation in the natural. When free moral agents submit their lives to the devil in any area, they have given territory to the kingdom of darkness. Most often, this is done unknowingly.

Darkness will hit you with an all-out assault on your emotions and experiences to get you to crack. By "crack," I mean to agree with any way of thinking that opposes the written Word of God. When you violate the written Word of God in your thinking or actions, you are now a territory the devil can operate through. However, through Jesus, His blood, and repentance, you can defeat that destructive access and territory by surrendering to Jesus and His words.

ORIGIN OF THE COSMIC BATTLE

Darkness doesn't play fair by our standards, but it must operate legally and spiritually. You outrank evil spirits and fallen angels. You have God's very breath in you, and you have a physical body. The only way you, as an individual, can lose to the powers of darkness is to give them permission to enter your life. This begins with your thought life. This is why we take every thought captive to the obedience of Jesus Christ!

For though we walk in the flesh, we do not war according to the flesh.[4] For the weapons of our warfare are not carnal but mighty in God for pulling down strongholds,[5] casting down arguments and every high thing that exalts itself against the knowledge of God, bringing every thought into captivity to the obedience of Christ,[6] and being ready to punish all disobedience when your obedience is fulfilled.
—2 Corinthians 10:3-6

Mind battles are one of the main points the scripture in 2 Corinthians 10 is referencing. Darkness pushes and pushes with thoughts and emotional manipulation until you cave in and agree with it, letting those thoughts take hold.

Beat the devil's prison rules and renew your mind to the written Word of God. When you do, two things will happen:

1. Access by darkness will be denied.
2. You will experience angelic cooperation by being a vessel for the Word of God to be released into the earth!

Chapter Four
Hell Is Not Enough

Then He will also say to those on the left hand, "Depart from Me, you cursed, into the everlasting fire prepared for the devil and his angels."

—Matthew 25:41

When it comes to the topic of hell and eternal punishment, the natural reaction by a thinking person is to ask often, *why?* Why would a loving God create such a horrible place? It seems over the top or unjust to many people to know individuals are in a place of unquenchable fire and burning in the most horrendous agony imaginable. Some can reconcile the thought of mean, vile people going to such a place, but not kind, ordinary people who lived decent lives. Any notion of an eternal hell could present a challenge to reconcile with the thoughts of loved ones, friends, or good people who may be headed there.

Hell is difficult to grapple with, especially when the truth of the matter is not presented correctly. Most people, even believers in Jesus, do not have a grasp of why such

ORIGIN OF THE COSMIC BATTLE

a severe eternal place would ever exist in the first place. Religion enters the narrative with *unhelpful tales or traditions* regarding hell. This only misconstrues information about why people go there or why, in some cases, there are exceptions for certain ones missing eternal damnation based on their good deeds.

Often, religion uses guilt and manipulation about hell to induce behavior modification, having little to do with the reality of the matter altogether. When talking about hell, I have found the most constructive point: Why was it formed in the first place? The answer might surprise you. When understanding eternal punishment, we must first realize that hell was not created for humanity. It was created for Lucifer and his band of rebellious fallen angels.

These rogue sons of God acted against God in the most heinous way imaginable. Their attempt to hijack what God loved most was an act of vengeance against Him for His choice to exalt man above their celestial station. Lucifer's mutiny was not only the highest treason ever committed, but it also caused an angelic chain reaction of further mutiny against God. For this reason, war broke out in heaven between Lucifer and his rogue forces in a collision with Michael, the archangel, and the forces of heaven. We will look into this topic more in the pages ahead, but first, let us come back to consider who God is.

The Perfection That Is God

God is pure light, and there is no darkness in Him. God is all good; there is no evil in Him. We as humans relegate sin as bad actions or behaviors with consequences. Although this is correct, it is certainly not a complete picture. To humanity, sin has rank and severity. One sin is not as bad as another.

An example would be telling a little white lie is not as bad in the eyes of most people as murdering someone is. Certain sins may be more grotesque than others to our natural minds and system of thinking. Humans typically judge things based on how we feel about what was done. A judgment involves our worldview, cultural norms, values, what is acceptable in society, and how our experiences shape what we believe to be good and evil. We grade on a curve based on subjective points of reference. Not God, because He is Spirit, as it says in John 4:24.

Sin Is Spiritual

God is holy, which doesn't mean He is only good and kind. He doesn't choose to be holy. Instead, *He is holiness personified*. God has no darkness in Him. God's holiness is spiritual perfection of the highest order. Compared to God, there is nothing higher in holiness and perfection. Nothing can compare to Him. God has no equal to make a standard of Himself against; all He has is His Word. This is why when He promised Abraham, He could swear by nothing greater, so He swore by Himself!

Understanding the heights of God's perfection and unparalleled holiness is the first step toward grasping *why hell exists and lasts forever.*

Hell was a reaction. As Newton's third law of motion says, "With every action, there is an equal and opposite reaction." This was the case regarding the spiritual violation of God's holiness! A reaction happened! However, there is nothing in all existence to rise as an equal to God's magnificence. A violation of God's holiness, by the mutiny of Lucifer, was the highest *spiritual violation* that had ever taken place! Think about it—this is why there will be a *new heaven and new earth*. Every place impacted by Lucifer's treachery will be done away with and recreated.

> *Then I saw a great white throne and Him who sat on it, from whose face the earth and the heaven fled away. And there was found no place for them.*
>
> —Revelation 20:11

> *Then He who sat on the throne said, "Behold, I make all things new." And He said to me, "Write, for these words are true and faithful."*
>
> —Revelation 21:5

Nevertheless we, according to His promise, look for new heavens and a new earth in which righteousness dwells.
—2 Peter 3:13

When the question is asked, "Why would a loving God send anyone to hell?" the immediate answer should be that God doesn't send anyone to hell. A proper response would be that if you knew the circumstances, you would recognize that God is a victim of a crime He chose to pay for! Additionally, hell is not enough. Furthermore, hell was not created for humanity! It is an angelic punishment. Yet, no matter how intensely and furiously hell burns, it will never suffice.

THE PUNISHMENT CANNOT PAY FOR THE CRIME

The devil, who deceived them, was cast into the lake of fire and brimstone where the beast and the false prophet are. And they will be tormented day and night forever and ever.

—Revelation 20:10

Indeed, the punishment is not enough to pay for the crime—this is why hell burns *forever*. There have been those who have made statements over the years that are contrary to what the Bible teaches, such as, "Hell will come to an end because of love," or eventually, hell will be stopped because of the love of God. However, it's not about what God desires or what His will is; it is about action, reaction, and spiritual law.

Might we suppose that God could have wiped out Adam and Eve the moment they sinned as a result of their listening to the serpent? If so, then God the Father would have lost His kids forever. Adam and Eve were God's kids; and they, along with creation itself, were (in a sense) taken hostage by Satan. How? When Adam and Eve chose the serpent's word over the Word of God, they immediately gave up the rights and authority they possessed to the one they chose to obey.

These two were to reign with dominion over the Garden and earth. Subduing all creation was one of the assignments in which they were designated to operate. Everything they had been entrusted with was given over to the devil. He now had the authority and access to walk with God in the cool of the day or present himself along with the sons of God. Satan took creation hostage through the original sin of Adam and Eve.

Rather than see His children destroyed, God chose to launch a rescue mission to save His family. It took hundreds of years of prophecy and obedience to see God's prophetic statement, "You will bruise His heel, but He will crush your head" (see Genesis 3:15). God decided to go after His family, even at the cost of being rejected. He chose to allow us to have a choice by sending Jesus.

There have been teachers and preachers who claim hell will not last for all eternity. Even if they mean well, they do not understand what the Scripture teaches. One day, thinking about these unbiblical claims, I realized they were right! Hell will not last forever. Sadly, and tragically, one day, hell and all its inhabitants will come to an end of sorts. This will happen the day hell, and *everything within it* is cast into the lake of fire. Now, saying hell will not last forever does not mean eternal punishment and damnation come to an end. Instead, the exact opposite is true. As horrifying as it is, damnation will increase in intensity and result in a heightened level of punishment that goes well beyond our capacity to understand.

> *Then Death and Hades were cast into the lake of fire. This is the second death.*
>
> —Revelation 20:14

The thought of this moment is dreadful and horrifying. Every time I read this Scripture; it makes me hurt for the Lord. The only thing He doesn't have is the lost. I don't know about you, but I want to honor the Lord by pursuing the lost and bringing them home to Him. Leading people to salvation is one of the greatest ways to glorify God!

The Lake of Fire Will Last Forever

And the smoke of their torment ascends forever and ever; and they have no rest day or night....

—Revelation 14:11

The lake of fire is called the "second death." Much of the reasoning behind this title is that it likely is far more impossible to describe than hell itself. Hell is a place we can locate scriptural descriptions—not as much regarding the lake of fire. Some say it might be that hell is cast into a star and suggest that is what the lake of fire is. Others suggest that this is a place beyond the outer darkness. It could be that the lake of fire is a spiritual location superseding all comprehension for human capacity. The term "second death" may allude to the *second level* of existence, removed from the spiritual realm of heaven and hell—twice removed from this natural planet we live on.

Another concept, in the realm of possibility, is that the term *second death* refers to the second level of removal from God. When considering a biblical studies term known as the law of first mention, we see that the first time death is referenced is regarding the tree in the Garden of Eden. When Adam and Eve disobeyed God, they died. These two did not collapse and die; instead, they were removed from the Garden and experienced a separation from God. So, death could be understood as a separation from God. Jesus came and bridged this gap and even reconciled man back to God.

In John 20:22, Jesus breathed on the disciples and said, "Receive the Holy Spirit"—an act that God the Father did in Genesis when breathing life into Adam. Jesus was reconnecting man to God; He breathed life into them. New life or salvation is also coming back from the dead with God. Lost people today are dead spiritually. They are separated from the Father God. If they die in that state, they will face death in eternity, and the first level is hell. The second death, the lake of fire, is to be twice removed from God the Father. Such a concept could refer to two dimensions, two realities, two levels of judgment, or two deaths away from the One true living God.

For I will be merciful to their unrighteousness, and their sins and their lawless deeds I will remember no more.
—Hebrews 8:12

He will again have compassion on us, and will subdue our iniquities. You will cast all our sins into the depths of the sea.
—Micah 7:19

In God's infinite mercy, could it also be that just as He remembers *our sin no more*, there will be very little memory of such a place as the lake of fire and those in it in eternity future? Any conclusion we might arrive at is conjecture at best. However, we do know that the reality of such a place is so terrible we cannot ascertain it. Knowing about hell is awful enough, but, likely, we could not grasp what the second death truly is as it relates to the lake of fire.

Hell in all its fury, the lake of fire raging forever and ever, is still not enough to pay for the crime against God's holiness. If you want to understand how holy and pure God is, then consider how horrible hell and the lake of fire are. Despite all the punishment they can muster, there still isn't enough to pay for the violation against God's holiness. God made a way for humankind to escape through Jesus. Some ask, "Why not the devil and his fallen angels, too? Why can't they have an opportunity to escape?" The reason is, they never had a tempter. Adam and Eve did.

Angels and celestial beings are spirits that cannot be destroyed. They will exist forever somewhere.

God, who knew the horrors that would await all who would not choose Him, went through the highest extremes to get us—He sent Jesus. God preferred to give humanity the choice of accepting or rejecting Him as an alternative to intentionally destroying Adam and Eve. The choice was presented to all creation rather than God deliberately leaving His son and daughter in the clutches of the devil for all eternity. What a thought! God chose to give humanity the choice to be with Him or live eternally separated forever, rather than permanently lose His first children by His choosing.

Hope and Salvation Through Jesus

There is good news—we never have to experience any of the terrible things we just read about regarding a crisis eternity! God desires each person to come to Him and avoid this horrible situation altogether. It is simple to run to our Creator. *God loves you!* Jesus came to seek and save all who are lost or on their way to a crisis eternity. If you want to receive Jesus and have eternal life starting today, please pray the following.

Pray This Prayer to Receive Jesus

Jesus, I believe You are the Son of God, that You died on the cross to rescue me from sin and an eternity apart from God. I believe God raised You from the dead. I believe You came to restore me to God the Father. I repent and choose to turn away from my sins. I give myself to You,

ORIGIN OF THE COSMIC BATTLE

trading my life for Your life. I receive Your forgiveness and ask You to become my Savior. Wash me by Your blood. I receive You completely! I declare Jesus is my Lord! Thank You, Lord. In Jesus' name, I pray. Amen.

If you prayed this prayer or helped someone else pray it, please contact our ministry, and we will send you free teaching about salvation!

Welcome to the family!

ABOUT JOSEPH Z

Joseph Z is a Bible teacher, author, broadcaster, and international prophetic voice. Before the age of nine, he began encountering the Voice of God through dreams and visions. This resulted in a journey that has led him to dedicate his life to preaching the gospel and teaching the Bible, often followed by prophetic ministry.

For nearly three decades, Joseph planted churches, founded Bible schools, preached stadium events, and held schools of the prophets around the world. Joseph and his wife, Heather, ministered together for 15 years and made the decision in 2012 to start Z Ministries, a media and conference-based ministry. During this time, they traveled the United States, taking along with them a traveling studio team, live broadcasting from a new location several times a week.

A season came when Heather became very ill due to hereditary kidney failure. After three years of dialysis and several miracles, she received a miracle kidney transplant. Joseph and Heather decided to stop everything, they laid everything down and ministered to their family for nearly three years.

ORIGIN OF THE COSMIC BATTLE

In 2017 Joseph had an encounter with the Lord and received the word to "go live every weekday morning"—Monday through Friday. What started with him, Heather, and a small group of viewers, has turned into a large and faithful online broadcast family. Today, his live broadcasts are reaching millions every month with the gospel and current events—which he has labeled "prophetic journalism." He additionally interviews some of the leading voices in the church, government, and the culture.

He and Heather have two adult children who faithfully work alongside them. Joseph's favorite saying when ending letters, books, or written articles is, "For Jesus." As, "For the testimony of Jesus is the spirit of prophecy" (Revelation 19:10).

Joseph spends his time with his family, writing books, broadcasting, and training others in the Word of God.

For Further Information

If you would like prayer or further
information about Joseph Z Ministries,
please call our offices at

(719) 257-8050 or visit **JosephZ.com/contact**

Visit JosephZ.com for additional materials.

From
JOSEPH Z

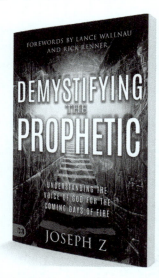

Navigate the End Times With Prophetic Precision

Never before have we had a greater need for clear, prophetic insight. Our world is teeming with widespread prophetic error, controversy, and deception—discrediting the legitimate prophetic voices God is using to speak to us. We need true biblical prophecy to take its place at the forefront of our lives.

Joseph Z, internationally respected prophetic voice, began encountering the Voice of God from a young age through dreams and visions. With wisdom, accuracy, biblical balance, and experience, Joseph offers powerful keys to help you unlock the revelation, interpretation, and application of prophecy.

The stakes have never been higher. Only true and refined prophecy cuts through the deception with unmatched power and precision. Both the Church and the world are in desperate need for this elevated prophetic encounter. Now, Jesus urgently seeks to equip you to navigate these critical last days with prophetic insight.

Purchase your copy wherever books are sold

From
JOSEPH Z

Thriving in God's Supernatural Economy

There's a war being fought over you! The Kingdom of God offers you divine provision while the Kingdom of Hell fights for territory in your life as a crisis looms on the world's horizon.

Will you break free of Hell's economy? International prophet and Bible teacher Joseph Z say it's urgent to break free now as we rapidly plunge into global difficulties involving worldwide market collapse, bank closures, a digital one-world currency, power grids failing, cyber war, medical deception, natural catastrophes, and unprecedented international conflict.

In *Breaking Hell's Economy*, Joseph makes it clear that we're at a destination in history that requires a revelation of God's supernatural economy—your ultimate defense against rising darkness.

Lay hold of this revelation, defy Hell, and live your life knowing you are destined to thrive in the last days!

Purchase your copy wherever books are sold

From
JOSEPH Z

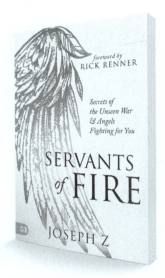

Deploying God's Angelic Army

In the realm of the spirit, invisible forces contend over the will of God for your life, but you are not alone in this fight. Warrior angels—servants of fire—have been sent to minister to you as an heir of salvation.

Joseph Z, Bible teacher and prophetic seer, reveals the role of God's angelic warriors who carry out the Word of God on your behalf.

Servants of Fire delivers sound biblical instruction to unveil the realm of the spirit and bring to pass the will, plans, and purposes of God on the earth.

Understand how to partner with these servants of fire so you can experience the maximum impact of a victorious life in God!

Purchase your copy wherever books are sold

Check out
our **Harrison House**
bestsellers page at
<u>harrisonhouse.com/bestsellers</u>

for fresh,
faith-building messages
that will equip you
to walk in the
abundant life.

In the Right Hands, This Book Will Change Lives!

Most of the people who need this message will not be looking for this book. To change their lives, you need to **put a copy of this book in their hands.**

Our ministry is constantly seeking methods to find the people who need this anointed message to change their lives. **Will you help us reach these people?**

Extend this ministry by sowing three, five, ten, or *even more* books today and change people's lives for the better! Your generosity will be part of catalyzing the Great Awakening that many have been prophesying and praying for.